Table of Contents

Emergency Vehicles   3

Photo Glossary   15

Index   16

About the Author   16

Can you find these words?

ambulance | fire engine

ladder | tow truck

Emergency Vehicles

People are in trouble. Help is on the way!

A **fire engine** fights fires.

fire engine

4

Water shoots from its hose.

ladder

A fire truck lifts its **ladder**.
Up! Up! Up!

7

An **ambulance** takes sick people to the hospital.

ambulance

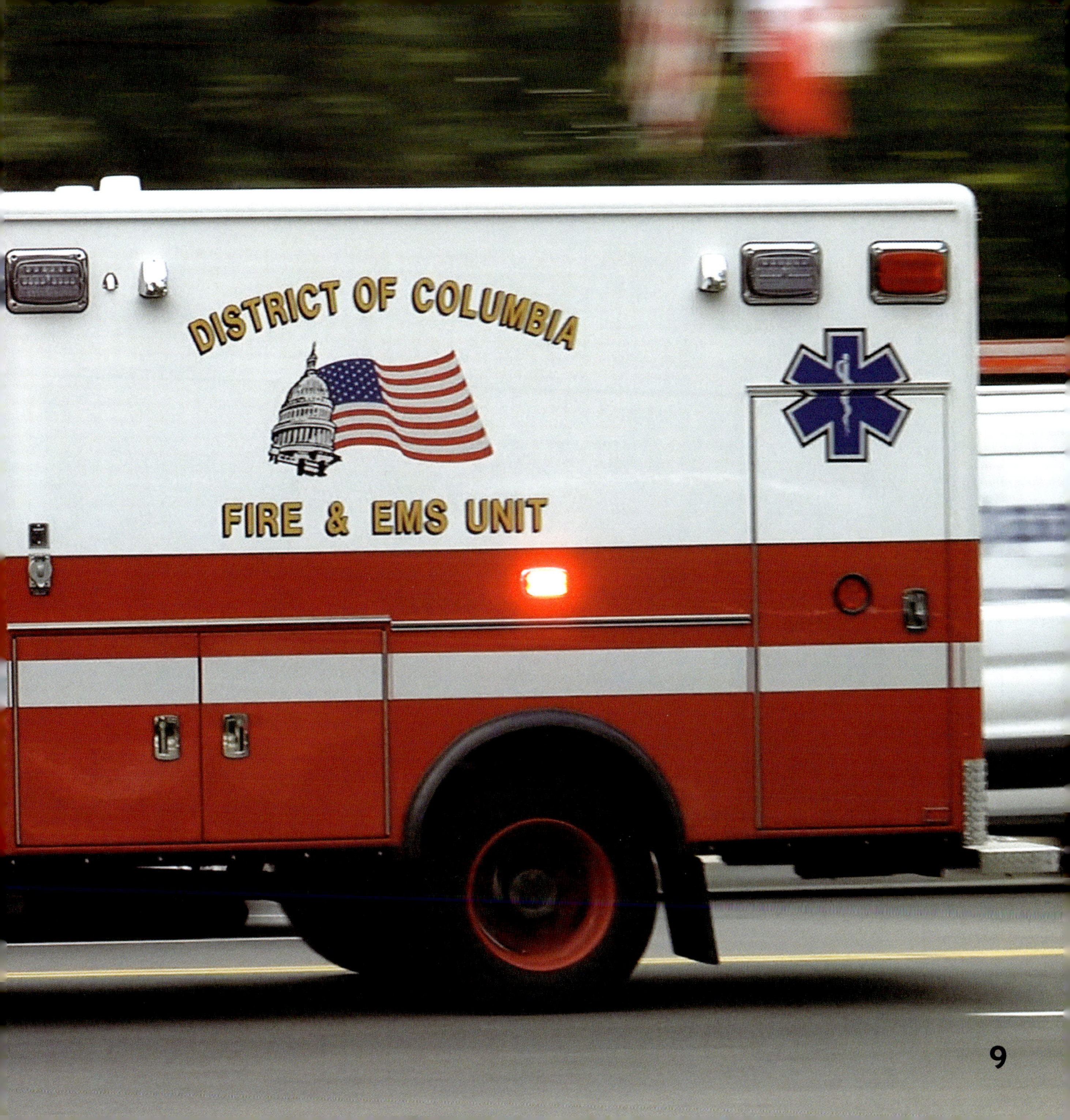
DISTRICT OF COLUMBIA
FIRE & EMS UNIT

A **tow truck** helps a broken car.

10

tow truck

Emergency vehicles get the job done!

Index

ambulance 8
fire engine 4
fire truck 6

hose 5
ladder 6
lifts 6

About the Author

Katy Duffield is an author who would like to drive a tow truck. She would like sitting tall in the big seat. She would like helping people, too. Mostly, she'd love pulling those cars around. And she'd probably even try out the horn. HONK!

© 2019 Rourke Educational Media

All rights reserved. No part of this book may be reproduced or utilized in any form or by any means, electronic or mechanical including photocopying, recording, or by any information storage and retrieval system without permission in writing from the publisher.

www.rourkeeducationalmedia.com

PHOTO CREDITS: ©MarkusBeck; p.2,8-9,14,15: ©bakdc; p.2,4-5,14,15: ©blurAZ; p.2,6-7,14,15: ©Fedecandoniphoto | Dreamstime.com; p.2,10-11,14,15: ©CrispyPork; p.3: ©Mark Bowden; p.12-13: &#169 Catherine Yeulet

Edited by: Keli Sipperley
Cover design by: Kathy Walsh
Interior design by: Rhea Magaro-Wallace

Library of Congress PCN Data
Emergency Vehicles / Katy Duffield
(My World)
ISBN (hard cover)(alk. paper) 978-1-64156-200-3
ISBN (soft cover) 978-1-64156-256-0
ISBN (e-Book) 978-1-64156-305-5
Library of Congress Control Number: 2017957809

Printed in the United States of America, North Mankato, Minnesota

Photo Glossary

ambulance (AM-byuh-luhns): A vehicle that takes sick or hurt people to the hospital.

fire engine (fire EN-juhn): A large vehicle with pumps that firefighters use to help put out fires.

ladder (LAD-ur): A structure made of steel, rope, or wood that is used to climb up and down.

tow truck (TOW truhk): A truck used to pull damaged or broken-down vehicles.

Did you find these words?

An **ambulance** takes sick people to the hospital.

A **fire engine** fights fires.

A fire truck lifts its **ladder**.

A **tow truck** helps a broken car.

13